Eye of Evil

Paul Jennings

This b·   be ·
t·

Stanley Thornes (Publishers) Ltd

14578

First published in 1986 by Hutchinson Education
Reprinted in 1987, 1989

Reprinted 1991 by
Stanley Thornes (Publishers) Ltd
Ellenborough House
Wellington Street
CHELTENHAM GL50 1YD
England

Reprinted 1994 (twice), 1995

British Library Cataloguing in Publication Data

Jennings, Paul
    Eye of evil. — (Spirals).
    I. Title   II. Series
    428.6'2   PE1126.A4

    ISBN 0 7487 1045 0

Basic Skills Collection

Cover photograph by Steve Richards.
Cover design by Martin Grant-Hudson
Printed and bound in Great Britain by Martin's The Printers, Berwick.

1

When I was sixteen I left school and got a job. I worked in a factory that made salt and pepper shakers.

It was a boring job. All I had to do was put the plugs into the bottom of salt and pepper shakers. There was a box of salt and pepper shakers and a box of plugs. I put them together and then threw them into another box.

The job didn't pay much. Forty pounds a week after tax. But beggars can't be choosers. Jobs were hard to get and it was better than being on the dole.

I was saving up to go on a trip. I wanted to see the world. To do that I needed money. Lots of money. So I kept at it. I hated the job but I kept working to get the money.

I had to work hard. Every day the workers had to finish one thousand pairs of salt and pepper shakers. That is a lot of salt and pepper shakers. If we didn't finish at least one thousand pairs we would get the sack.

As I said before, it was boring. Salt and pepper shakers are not very interesting. When you've seen one, you've seen them all.

Three other people worked with me. We all spent every day putting the plugs into salt and pepper shakers. We all became good friends.

The name of the boss was Pollock. He was the foreman. He was a big man with a red face. He had one glass eye. He had lost the real one in a fight in a pub.

One of the other workers was about my age. His name was George. I didn't know much about George because he couldn't talk. He could hear but he couldn't say anything. He would nod and point at things but never speak. He smiled a lot. He was nearly always smiling and whistling.

George wasn't very smart. He believed everything he was told. Because of this people were always playing tricks on him. Once Pollock played a dirty trick on George. He wrote a note out for George to take down to the shops. On the note it said: 'Please sell George one sky hook.'

There is no such thing as a sky hook. You can't hang a hook on the sky but George didn't know this. He went to about twenty shops. All the shopkeepers laughed at him and told him to try somewhere else.

In the end he was told that there is no such thing as a sky hook. George was very upset. He had spent all day walking around looking for something that didn't exist. He didn't smile and whistle much that day.

Pollock was a dirty rat. The four of us all hated him. But he was the foreman. You had to do what he said.

2

Two other men worked with George and me. There was Ralph, who was an old man, and Joe, who was about forty.

Ralph was a slow worker. He found it hard to keep up with the work. One thousand pairs of salt and pepper shakers was the number we had to do. He had to finish his share just like the rest of us.

Pollock didn't care that Ralph was old. He didn't care that Ralph had sore fingers and his joints were stiff. He made Ralph finish his share every day.

Poor old Ralph. At the end of the day his fingers were so stiff that he could hardly move them.

Joe was a quick worker. He could finish two thousand pairs in a day if he wanted to. He never did of course. He watched the clock. At five o'clock he had always finished one thousand pairs exactly. No more, no less.

This used to make Pollock angry. He knew that Joe could do more work but there was nothing that he could do about it. The number was one thousand pairs a day and Joe always finished his share.

Joe had six kids. He needed the money badly. He spent all of his wages on food and clothes for the kids. On pay day he gave his pay packet to his wife. He never had any money left for himself. His family was very poor.

We all needed the money. That's why we put up with Pollock. We were scared of getting the sack. We did what Pollock told us even though he was a ratbag.

3

Pollock was always trying to think of new ways to make us work harder. He would watch us while we worked. He wouldn't let us talk or smoke on the job. It was such a boring job that we needed to talk. It made the time go more quickly.

Pollock couldn't watch us all day. He had to go into the office sometimes. When Pollock wasn't there we talked. We talked, told jokes and laughed. We kept working but we had a good time as well.

This used to make Pollock cross. He tried to catch us talking but he never could. He used to sneak up behind us but we always saw him coming.

One day Pollock put up a glass case on the wall where we worked. We didn't know what he was up to. He had a nasty smile on his face.

'Boys,' he said, 'from now on I'm going to watch you all the time. Even when I'm not here. You won't be able to talk because I'll be watching you all day.'

He looked at George and grinned. 'I'm going to keep an eye on you, George.'

Then he took out his glass eye and put it in the case. He closed the case door and locked it.

The glass eye was looking at us from the case on the wall. Pollock took an eye patch out of his pocket and put it over his empty eye. He looked like a pirate with his patch on.

'George, you'd better work hard,' said Pollock. 'This eye is watching you. It can see everything you do. From now on I'll know what you are doing when I'm not here.'

Pollock went off to the office with a big smirk on his face. He thought it was a great joke.

Ralph, Joe and I couldn't believe it. We knew it was just a glass eye. It couldn't see anything. Who did he think he was fooling?

The glass eye just sat there. It looked like it was watching us but it was only a glass eye.

4

That glass eye caused a lot of trouble. George was scared of it. He was frightened out of his wits. He thought it was alive and staring at him. He kept looking up at it. He thought that Pollock could see what he was doing.

George began to work very fast. He didn't stop for lunch. He worked all day without stopping.

We tried to tell him that it was a trick like the sky hook. But it wasn't any use. He just pointed to the eye and worked even harder.

At the end of the day George finished more than two thousand pairs of salt and pepper shakers. He was so tired he could hardly stand up.

Pollock was very pleased. 'Good work, George,' he said. 'You're working much better now the eye is watching you. The eye will be back tomorrow and I'll know how hard you're working.'

Every day that week George finished more and more pairs of salt and pepper shakers. He was frightened

of that eye. It had him fooled. On the Friday of that
week he finished three thousand pairs.

George was beginning to get thin. He was losing
weight. Working so hard and not eating wasn't good
for his health.

On the next Monday Pollock called us together for a
talk. 'Men,' he said, 'On Friday George finished three
thousand pairs. This shows what you can do if you
work hard. If he can finish three thousand pairs you
can all finish three thousand pairs. From now on you
must all finish three thousand pairs every day.'

'That's too many,' said Ralph. 'I can't do that
many. I'm too old and my fingers hurt.'

'Too bad,' replied Pollock. 'If you don't finish three
thousand every day you'll get the sack.'

He took out his glass eye and put it in the
case. Then he went off laughing.

'He can't do it,' I said. 'We should tell the
union. The union won't let him do it.'

'If we tell the union,' said Joe, 'they'll call a strike. If
we go on strike we won't get any pay. Who'll feed
my kids if we don't have any pay? Will you?'

We had no choice. We had to try and finish three thousand a day or get the sack.

We were angry with Pollock. We were also angry with George. It was all his fault. If he hadn't worked so hard this would never have happened.

That stupid eye was still in the case. It stared out at us. It didn't care about our trouble. After all, it belonged to Pollock.

5

That day I finished my three thousand pairs. So did George and Joe. But not Ralph. He couldn't keep up. His fingers hurt. As the day went by he went more and more slowly. He was too old for such hard work.

At the end of the day Ralph had only finished one thousand five hundred pairs.

Pollock came down to get his glass eye and check our work. He looked at Ralph's work and said, 'This isn't good enough, Ralph. You'll have to go. You're sacked. You can stay until Friday but after that you can't come back.'

Ralph was upset. Tears rolled down his wrinkled face. 'I won't be able to get another job,' he said. 'I'm too old.'

'That's right,' replied Pollock. 'We need a young man here too. I'll give your job to a younger man who can do more work. You should be glad to see a young person get a chance.'

'I won't be able to pay the rent,' said Ralph. 'They'll put me in a home for old people.'

He shuffled off. He looked very, very old.

Pollock didn't care. 'You other men had better watch your step too,' was all he said. 'Or the same thing will happen to you.'

I was angry with George. After Pollock left I started to yell at him. 'This is all your fault, George. You and that damned eye. If you hadn't worked so fast Ralph would still have his job. Now they'll put Ralph in an old folks' home. He'll just give up and die. And it will be your fault. You'll probably get us all the sack.'

I shouldn't have said all this but I was angry. I felt sorry for poor old Ralph.

George began to cry. He didn't make any noise but tears rolled down his face. His shoulders shook silently. I went out and left him crying.

6

We were all unhappy on the next day. We worked without talking. There was nothing to say. Ralph had to leave on Friday. Nothing was going to cheer him up.

The glass eye sat in its case. George kept looking at it. He was still scared of it and he worked hard because he thought it could see him.

Joe, Ralph and I stopped for lunch at twelve-thirty. George kept working as usual. We left him there and went to the lunch room.

While we were eating our sandwiches, Ralph said to me, 'I think you should get George. It's not his fault that I'm getting the sack. He's scared of the eye. It's Pollock's fault, not George's. Tell him to come and have some lunch.'

I went back to get George but what I saw made me stop. The glass case was broken and the eye was gone. George was kneeling on the floor. His face was white and his hands were trembling.

In front of him was a brick. On the brick was the

glass eye. George hit it with a hammer. He hit it again and again. He had gone crazy. He smashed the glass eye into a million bits.

After a while he stopped and picked up a brush. He swept all the pieces into a paper bag and put the bag in his pocket. Then he went back to work.

I went slowly back to the lunch room. I didn't tell anyone what I'd seen. I didn't let George know that I knew his secret.

After lunch Ralph and Joe were shocked to see that the glass eye had gone. 'There'll be trouble now,' said Ralph. 'Pollock will be mad when he finds that his precious eye has gone.'

Pollock *was* mad. He was furious. His face went purple. 'I want that eye back,' he shouted. 'Who took it?'

No one answered. He glared at George. 'Did you see who took it, George?'

George didn't say anything. He couldn't speak even if he wanted to. He just shook his head.

A little later Pollock came back with the Big Boss. His real name was Mr Sharp. He owned the factory. He didn't come into the workshop very often. Only when something was wrong. We always called him the Big Boss when he couldn't hear.

'Listen, men,' said Mr Sharp. 'Something bad has happened. Someone has stolen Mr Pollock's glass eye. This is a serious crime. That glass eye cost a lot of money. Mr Pollock left his eye in the washroom and someone has taken it.'

We could tell Mr Sharp didn't know that Pollock left the eye in the case to frighten George. He didn't know what a rat Pollock was.

'If that eye isn't back by tomorrow morning,' he went on, 'all of you men will get the sack. I'm not going to have a thief in this factory.'

Mr Sharp stared straight at Ralph when he said this. I think he blamed Ralph. He must have thought that Ralph did it to get back at Pollock. To get revenge.

I looked at George. He looked ill. He looked as if he was going to faint.

7

After Mr Sharp had gone there was a row. A big
argument. Joe thought that Ralph had taken the
eye. 'Give it back, Ralph,' he said. 'We'll all get the
sack if you don't.'

'I didn't touch the rotten eye,' replied Ralph. 'I was at
lunch when it went.'

We were all upset. Ralph was already sacked and
the rest of us were going to get the sack too. The
eye wouldn't be put back. It couldn't be put back
because it was smashed into a million pieces.

I didn't tell anyone that George had done it. He
would have to own up. It was not up to me to say
anything.

George was very pale. His lips were trembling. He
looked as if he was going to cry. He knew that we
were going to lose our jobs because of what he'd
done.

We all went home in a bad mood that night.

8

The next morning something strange happened. The eye was back! There it was sitting in the broken case staring at us.

Where had it come from? George had smashed it with a hammer. How could it be back in the case?

Someone must have got another glass eye and put it there. I looked at it closely. It was the right colour. It looked just the same to me. I wondered if Pollock would know that it was a different eye.

I hoped that Pollock would think that it was the same eye. I didn't want to get the sack. Neither did Joe. Joe looked very happy to see the glass eye back in its case.

Later that morning Mr Sharp came down to see us. He had a policeman with him.

'Something terrible has happened,' said Mr Sharp. 'Mr Pollock is dead. He has been murdered. His body has been found at the back of the factory.'

Then he said something that made us shiver. 'His

body has no eyes. The glass eye has gone and so has the other one.' I rushed over to the case and looked at the eye. I thought that I saw it wobble. It seemed to be glaring at George.

George was still working at those salt and pepper shakers. He was working slowly. He didn't care about the eye any more. He didn't care about anything. Not even the man in blue who walked towards him. With a pair of handcuffs.

Stories in the spirals series

Anita Jackson
The Actor
The Ear
The Austin Seven
Dreams
Bennet Manor
Pentag
No Rent to Pay
Doctor Maxwell
A Game of Life or Death

Jim Alderston
The Witch Princess
Crash in the Jungle

Jan Carew
Death Comes to the Circus

Susan Duberley
The Ring

**Keith Fletcher and
Susan Duberley**
Nightmare Lake

Paul Groves
The Third Climber

Paul Jennings
Eye of Evil
Maggot

Kevin Philbin
Summer of the Werewolf

John Townsend
Fame and Fortune
Beware the Morris Minor

Plays

Jan Carew
Time Loop
  Two short plays for seven to eight parts
No Entry
  Two short plays for seven to eight parts
Computer Killer
  Two short plays for six to seven parts

John Godfrey
When I Count to Three
  Three short plays for five to six parts

Nigel Gray
An Earwig in the Ear
  Three short plays for two parts

Paul Groves
Tell Me Where it Hurts
  Three short plays for two to five parts

Barbara Mitchelhill
Punchlines
  Six short plays for two to four parts
The Ramsbottoms at Home
  Three plays for four and five parts

Madeline Sotheby
Hard Times at Batwing Hall
  Two short plays for four to five parts

John Townsend
The End of the Line
  One play for a larger group
Taking the Plunge
  Three short plays for up to four parts
Cheer and Groan
  Two short plays for four parts
Hanging by a Fred
  One play for a larger group
Making a Splash
  Three short plays for two to four parts
Murder at Muckleby Manor
  One play for a larger group
Over and Out
  Two short plays for two parts

David Walke
The Good, the Bad and the Bungle
  Three short plays for three parts
Package Holiday
  Three short plays for four parts
The Bungle Gang Strikes Again
  Three short plays for four to six parts